Police and Criminal Evidence Act 1984 (PACE)

CODE B
Revised

CODE OF PRACTICE FOR SEARCHES OF PREMISES BY POLICE OFFICERS AND THE SEIZURE OF PROPERTY FOUND BY POLICE OFFICERS ON PERSONS OR PREMISES

October 2013.

Commencement - Transitional Arrangements

This Code applies to applications for warrants made after 00.00 on 27 October 2013 and to searches and seizures taking place after 00.00 on 27 October 2013.

GRAN*GIS* UK Publishing

Adapted and Published by GRANGIS (Grand Register Library).
Online: www.grangis.com.
E-mail: contact@grangis.com.

© GRANGIS 2022.
In this version:
ISBN: 979-8-88559-090-7
Where we have identified any copyrighted material, you will need to obtain written permission for re-use.
Note: Title, sub-title and version of this publication is as described. For the most recent information please visit www.gov.uk.

Contents

1   Introduction

1.1   This Code of Practice deals with police powers to:

- search premises

- seize and retain property found on premises and persons

1.1A   These powers may be used to find:

- property and material relating to a crime

- wanted persons

- children who abscond from local authority accommodation where they have been remanded or committed by a court

1.2   A justice of the peace may issue a search warrant granting powers of entry, search and seizure, e.g. warrants to search for stolen property, drugs, firearms and evidence of serious offences. Police also have powers without a search warrant. The main ones provided by the Police and Criminal Evidence Act 1984 (PACE) include powers to search premises:

- to make an arrest

- after an arrest

1.3   The right to privacy and respect for personal property are key principles of the Human Rights Act 1998. Powers of entry, search and seizure should be fully and clearly justified before use because they may significantly interfere with the occupier's privacy. Officers should consider if the necessary objectives can be met by less intrusive means.

1.3A   Powers to search and seize must be used fairly, responsibly, with respect for people who occupy premises being searched or are in charge of property being seized and without unlawful discrimination. Under the Equality Act 2010, section 149, when police officers are carrying out their functions, they also have a duty to have due regard to the need to eliminate unlawful discrimination, harassment and victimisation, to advance equality of opportunity between people who share a relevant protected characteristic and people who do not share it, and to take steps to foster good relations between those persons. See *Note 1A*.

1.4   In all cases, police should therefore:

- exercise their powers courteously and with respect for persons and property

- only use reasonable force when this is considered necessary and proportionate to the circumstances

1.5   If the provisions of PACE and this Code are not observed, evidence obtained from a search may be open to question.

Note for Guidance

1A   In paragraph 1.3A, 'relevant protected characteristic' includes: age, disability, gender reassignment, pregnancy and maternity, race, religion/belief, sex and sexual orientation.

2 General

2.1 This Code must be readily available at all police stations for consultation by:

- police officers
- police staff
- detained persons
- members of the public

2.2 The *Notes for Guidance* included are not provisions of this Code.

2.3 This Code applies to searches of premises:

(a) by police for the purposes of an investigation into an alleged offence, with the occupier's consent, other than:

  - routine scene of crime searches;
  - calls to a fire or burglary made by or on behalf of an occupier or searches following the activation of fire or burglar alarms or discovery of insecure premises;
  - searches when *paragraph 5.4* applies;
  - bomb threat calls;

(b) under powers conferred on police officers by PACE, sections 17, 18 and 32;

(c) undertaken in pursuance of search warrants issued to and executed by constables in accordance with PACE, sections 15 and 16 (see *Note 2A*);

(d) subject to *paragraph 2.6*, under any other power given to police to enter premises with or without a search warrant for any purpose connected with the investigation into an alleged or suspected offence. (See *Note 2B.*)

For the purposes of this Code, 'premises' as defined in PACE, section 23, includes any place, vehicle, vessel, aircraft, hovercraft, tent or movable structure and any offshore installation as defined in the Mineral Workings (Offshore Installations) Act 1971, section 1. (See *Note 2D.*)

2.4 A person who has not been arrested but is searched during a search of premises should be searched in accordance with Code A. (See *Note 2C.*)

2.5 This Code does not apply to the exercise of a statutory power to enter premises or to inspect goods, equipment or procedures if the exercise of that power is not dependent on the existence of grounds for suspecting that an offence may have been committed and the person exercising the power has no reasonable grounds for such suspicion.

2.6 This Code does not affect any directions or requirements of a search warrant, order or other power to search and seize lawfully exercised in England or Wales that any item or evidence seized under that warrant, order or power be handed over to a police force, court, tribunal, or other authority outside England or Wales. For example, warrants and orders issued in Scotland or Northern Ireland (see *Note 2B(f)*) and search warrants and powers provided for in sections 14 to 17 of the Crime (International Co-operation) Act 2003.

2.7   When this Code requires the prior authority or agreement of an officer of at least inspector or superintendent rank, that authority may be given by a sergeant or chief inspector authorised to perform the functions of the higher rank under PACE, section 107.

2.8   Written records required under this Code not made in the search record shall, unless otherwise specified, be made:

- in the recording officer's pocket book ('pocket book' includes any official report book issued to police officers) or

- on forms provided for the purpose

2.9   Nothing in this Code requires the identity of officers, or anyone accompanying them during a search of premises, to be recorded or disclosed:

(a)   in the case of enquiries linked to the investigation of terrorism; or

(b)   if officers reasonably believe recording or disclosing their names might put them in danger.

In these cases officers should use warrant or other identification numbers and the name of their police station. Police staff should use any identification number provided to them by the police force. (See *Note 2E.*)

2.10   The 'officer in charge of the search' means the officer assigned specific duties and responsibilities under this Code. Whenever there is a search of premises to which this Code applies one officer must act as the officer in charge of the search. (See *Note 2F.*)

2.11   In this Code:

(a)   'designated person' means a person other than a police officer, designated under the Police Reform Act 2002, Part 4 who has specified powers and duties of police officers conferred or imposed on them. (See *Note 2G.*)

(b)   any reference to a police officer includes a designated person acting in the exercise or performance of the powers and duties conferred or imposed on them by their designation.

(c)   a person authorised to accompany police officers or designated persons in the execution of a warrant has the same powers as a constable in the execution of the warrant and the search and seizure of anything related to the warrant. These powers must be exercised in the company and under the supervision of a police officer. (See *Note 3C.*)

2.12   If a power conferred on a designated person:

(a)   allows reasonable force to be used when exercised by a police officer, a designated person exercising that power has the same entitlement to use force;

(b)   includes power to use force to enter any premises, that power is not exercisable by that designated person except:

(i)   in the company and under the supervision of a police officer; or

(ii)   for the purpose of:

- saving life or limb; or

- preventing serious damage to property.

2.13   Designated persons must have regard to any relevant provisions of the Codes of Practice.

Notes for guidance

2A *PACE sections 15 and 16 apply to all search warrants issued to and executed by constables under any enactment, e.g. search warrants issued by a:*

   (a) *justice of the peace under the:*

- *Theft Act 1968, section 26 - stolen property;*
- *Misuse of Drugs Act 1971, section 23 - controlled drugs;*
- *PACE, section 8 - evidence of an indictable offence;*
- *Terrorism Act 2000, Schedule 5, paragraph 1;*
- *Terrorism Prevention and Investigation Measures Act 2011, Schedule 5, paragraph 8(2)(b) search of premises for compliance purposes (see paragraph 10.1).*

   (b) *Circuit judge under:*

- *PACE, Schedule 1;*
- *Terrorism Act 2000, Schedule 5, paragraph 11.*

2B *Examples of the other powers in paragraph 2.3(d) include:*

   (a) *Road Traffic Act 1988, section 6E(1) giving police power to enter premises under section 6E(1) to:*

- require a person to provide a specimen of breath; or
- arrest a person following:
    - ~ a positive breath test;
    - ~ failure to provide a specimen of breath;

   (b) *Transport and Works Act 1992, section 30(4) giving police powers to enter premises mirroring the powers in (a) in relation to specified persons working on transport systems to which the Act applies;*

   (c) *Criminal Justice Act 1988, section 139B giving police power to enter and search school premises for offensive weapons, bladed or pointed articles;*

   (d) *Terrorism Act 2000, Schedule 5, paragraphs 3 and 15 empowering a superintendent in urgent cases to give written authority for police to enter and search premises for the purposes of a terrorist investigation;*

   (e) *Explosives Act 1875, section 73(b) empowering a superintendent to give written authority for police to enter premises, examine and search them for explosives;*

   (f) *search warrants and production orders or the equivalent issued in Scotland or Northern Ireland endorsed under the Summary Jurisdiction (Process) Act 1881 or the Petty Sessions (Ireland) Act 1851 respectively for execution in England and Wales.*

   (g) *Terrorism Prevention and Investigation Measures Act 2011, Schedule 5, paragraphs 5(1), 6(2)(b) and 7(2), searches relating to TPIM notices (see paragraph 10.1).*

2C   *The Criminal Justice Act 1988, section 139B provides that a constable who has reasonable grounds to suspect an offence under the Criminal Justice Act 1988, section 139A or 139AAhas or is being committed may enter school premises and search the premises and any persons on the premises for any bladed or pointed article or offensive weapon. Persons may be searched under a warrant issued under the Misuse of Drugs Act 1971, section 23(3) to search premises for drugs or documents only if the warrant specifically authorises the search of persons on the premises. Powers to search premises under certain terrorism provisions also authorise the search of persons on the premises, for example, under paragraphs 1, 2, 11 and 15 of Schedule 5 to the Terrorism Act 2000 and section 52 of the Anti-terrorism, Crime and Security Act 2001.*

2D   *The Immigration Act 1971, Part III and Schedule 2 gives immigration officers powers to enter and search premises, seize and retain property, with and without a search warrant. These are similar to the powers available to police under search warrants issued by a justice of the peace and without a warrant under PACE, sections 17, 18, 19 and 32 except they only apply to specified offences under the Immigration Act 1971 and immigration control powers. For certain types of investigations and enquiries these powers avoid the need for the Immigration Service to rely on police officers becoming directly involved. When exercising these powers, immigration officers are required by the Immigration and Asylum Act 1999, section 145 to have regard to this Code's corresponding provisions. When immigration officers are dealing with persons or property at police stations, police officers should give appropriate assistance to help them discharge their specific duties and responsibilities.*

2E   *The purpose of paragraph 2.9(b) is to protect those involved in serious organised crime investigations or arrests of particularly violent suspects when there is reliable information that those arrested or their associates may threaten or cause harm to the officers or anyone accompanying them during a search of premises. In cases of doubt, an officer of inspector rank or above should be consulted.*

2F   *For the purposes of paragraph 2.10, the officer in charge of the search should normally be the most senior officer present. Some exceptions are:*

    (a)   a supervising officer who attends or assists at the scene of a premises search may appoint an officer of lower rank as officer in charge of the search if that officer is:

- *more conversant with the facts;*
- *a more appropriate officer to be in charge of the search;*

    (b)   when all officers in a premises search are the same rank. The supervising officer if available, must make sure one of them is appointed officer in charge of the search, otherwise the officers themselves must nominate one of their number as the officer in charge;

    (c)   a senior officer assisting in a specialist role. This officer need not be regarded as having a general supervisory role over the conduct of the search or be appointed or expected to act as the officer in charge of the search.

Except in (c), nothing in this Note diminishes the role and responsibilities of a supervisory officer who is present at the search or knows of a search taking place.

2G   *An officer of the rank of inspector or above may direct a designated investigating officer not to wear a uniform for the purposes of a specific operation.*

3 Search warrants and production orders

(a) Before making an application

3.1 When information appears to justify an application, the officer must take reasonable steps to check the information is accurate, recent and not provided maliciously or irresponsibly. An application may not be made on the basis of information from an anonymous source if corroboration has not been sought. (See *Note 3A*.)

3.2 The officer shall ascertain as specifically as possible the nature of the articles concerned and their location.

3.3 The officer shall make reasonable enquiries to:

(i) establish if:

- anything is known about the likely occupier of the premises and the nature of the premises themselves;

- the premises have been searched previously and how recently;

(ii) obtain any other relevant information.

3.4 An application:

(a) to a justice of the peace for a search warrant or to a Circuit judge for a search warrant or production order under PACE, Schedule 1 must be supported by a signed written authority from an officer of inspector rank or above:

Note: If the case is an urgent application to a justice of the peace and an inspector or above is not readily available, the next most senior officer on duty can give the written authority.

(b) to a circuit judge under the Terrorism Act 2000, Schedule 5 for:

- a production order;

- search warrant; or

- an order requiring an explanation of material seized or produced under such a warrant or production order,

- must be supported by a signed written authority from an officer of superintendent rank or above.

3.5 Except in a case of urgency, if there is reason to believe a search might have an adverse effect on relations between the police and the community, the officer in charge shall consult the local police/community liaison officer:

- before the search; or

- in urgent cases, as soon as practicable after the search.

(b) Making an application

3.6 A search warrant application must be supported in writing, specifying:

(a) the enactment under which the application is made (see *Note 2A*);

(b) (i) whether the warrant is to authorise entry and search of:

- one set of premises; or

- if the application is under PACE section 8, or Schedule 1, paragraph 12, more than one set of specified premises or all premises occupied or controlled by a specified person, and

(ii) the premises to be searched;

(c) the object of the search (see *Note 3B*);

(d) the grounds for the application, including, when the purpose of the proposed search is to find evidence of an alleged offence, an indication of how the evidence relates to the investigation;

(da) Where the application is under PACE section 8, or Schedule 1, paragraph 12 for a single warrant to enter and search:

(i) more than one set of specified premises; the officer must specify each set of premises which it is desired to enter and search;

(ii) all premises occupied or controlled by a specified person; the officer must specify;

- as many sets of premises which it is desired to enter and search as it is reasonably practicable to specify;

- the person who is in occupation or control of those premises and any others which it is desired to search;

- why it is necessary to search more premises than those which can be specified, and

- why it is not reasonably practicable to specify all the premises which it is desired to enter and search;

(db) Whether an application under PACE section 8 is for a warrant authorising entry and search on more than one occasion, and if so, the officer must state the grounds for this and whether the desired number of entries authorised is unlimited or a specified maximum;

(e) That there are no reasonable grounds to believe the material to be sought, when making application to a:

(i) justice of the peace or a Circuit judge consists of or includes items subject to legal privilege;

(ii) justice of the peace, consists of or includes excluded material or special procedure material;

Note: this does not affect the additional powers of seizure in the Criminal Justice and Police Act 2001, Part 2 covered in *paragraph 7.7* (see *Note 3B*).

(f) if applicable, a request for the warrant to authorise a person or persons to accompany the officer who executes the warrant. (See *Note 3C*.)

3.7   A search warrant application under PACE, Schedule 1, paragraph 12(a), shall if appropriate indicate why it is believed service of notice of an application for a production order may seriously prejudice the investigation. Applications for search warrants under the Terrorism Act 2000, Schedule 5, paragraph 11 must indicate why a production order would not be appropriate.

3.8   If a search warrant application is refused, a further application may not be made for those premises unless supported by additional grounds.

Notes for guidance

3A   The identity of an informant need not be disclosed when making an application, but the officer should be prepared to answer any questions the magistrate or judge may have about:

- *the accuracy of previous information from that source, and*

- *any other related matters*

3B   The information supporting a search warrant application should be as specific as possible, particularly in relation to the articles or persons being sought and where in the premises it is suspected they may be found. The meaning of 'items subject to legal privilege', 'excluded material' and 'special procedure material' are defined by PACE, sections 10, 11 and 14 respectively.

3C   Under PACE, section 16(2), a search warrant may authorise persons other than police officers to accompany the constable who executes the warrant. This includes, e.g. any suitably qualified or skilled person or an expert in a particular field whose presence is needed to help accurately identify the material sought or to advise where certain evidence is most likely to be found and how it should be dealt with. It does not give them any right to force entry, but it gives them the right to be on the premises during the search and to search for or seize property without the occupier's permission.

4   Entry without warrant - particular powers

(a) Making an arrest etc

4.1   The conditions under which an officer may enter and search premises without a warrant are set out in PACE, section 17. It should be noted that this section does not create or confer any powers of arrest. See other powers in *Note 2B(a)*.

(b) Search of premises where arrest takes place or the arrested person was immediately before arrest

4.2   When a person has been arrested for an indictable offence, a police officer has power under PACE, section 32 to search the premises where the person was arrested or where the person was immediately before being arrested.

(c) Search of premises occupied or controlled by the arrested person

4.3   The specific powers to search premises which <u>are</u> occupied or controlled by a person arrested for an indictable offence are set out in PACE, section 18. They may not be exercised, except if section 18(5) applies, unless an officer of inspector rank or above has given written authority. That authority should only be given when the authorising officer is satisfied that the premises <u>are</u> occupied or controlled by the arrested person and that the necessary grounds exist. If possible the authorising officer should record the authority on the Notice of Powers and Rights and, subject to *paragraph 2.9*, sign the

Notice. The record of the grounds for the search and the nature of the evidence sought as required by section 16(7) of the Act should be made in:

- the custody record if there is one, otherwise

- the officer's pocket book, or

- the search record.

5 Search with consent

5.1   Subject to *paragraph 5.4*, if it is proposed to search premises with the consent of a person entitled to grant entry the consent must, if practicable, be given in writing on the Notice of Powers and Rights before the search. The officer must make any necessary enquiries to be satisfied the person is in a position to give such consent. (See *Notes 5A and 5B*.)

5.2   Before seeking consent the officer in charge of the search shall state the purpose of the proposed search and its extent. This information must be as specific as possible, particularly regarding the articles or persons being sought and the parts of the premises to be searched. The person concerned must be clearly informed they are not obliged to consent, that any consent given can be withdrawn at any time, including before the search starts or while it is underway and anything seized may be produced in evidence. If at the time the person is not suspected of an offence, the officer shall say this when stating the purpose of the search.

5.3   An officer cannot enter and search or continue to search premises under *paragraph 5.1* if consent is given under duress or withdrawn before the search is completed.

5.4   It is unnecessary to seek consent under *paragraphs 5.1* and *5.2* if this would cause disproportionate inconvenience to the person concerned. (See *Note 5C*.)

Notes for guidance

5A   *In a lodging house, hostel or similar accommodation, every reasonable effort should be made to obtain the consent of the tenant, lodger or occupier. A search should not be made solely on the basis of the landlord's consent.*

5B   *If the intention is to search premises under the authority of a warrant or a power of entry and search without warrant, and the occupier of the premises co-operates in accordance with paragraph 6.4, there is no need to obtain written consent.*

5C   *Paragraph 5.4 is intended to apply when it is reasonable to assume innocent occupiers would agree to, and expect, police to take the proposed action, e.g. if:*

- *a suspect has fled the scene of a crime or to evade arrest and it is necessary quickly to check surrounding gardens and readily accessible places to see if the suspect is hiding, or*

- *police have arrested someone in the night after a pursuit and it is necessary to make a brief check of gardens along the pursuit route to see if stolen or incriminating articles have been discarded.*

6 Searching premises - general considerations

(a) Time of searches

6.1 Searches made under warrant must be made within three calendar months of the date the warrant is issued or within the period specified in the enactment under which the warrant is issued if this is shorter.

6.2 Searches must be made at a reasonable hour unless this might frustrate the purpose of the search.

6.3 When the extent or complexity of a search mean it is likely to take a long time, the officer in charge of the search may consider using the seize and sift powers referred to in *section 7.*

6.3A A warrant under PACE, section 8 may authorise entry to and search of premises on more than one occasion if, on the application, the justice of the peace is satisfied that it is necessary to authorise multiple entries in order to achieve the purpose for which the warrant is issued. No premises may be entered or searched on any subsequent occasions without the prior written authority of an officer of the rank of inspector who is not involved in the investigation. All other warrants authorise entry on one occasion only.

6.3B Where a warrant under PACE section 8, or Schedule 1, paragraph 12 authorises entry to and search of all premises occupied or controlled by a specified person, no premises which are not specified in the warrant may be entered and searched without the prior written authority of an officer of the rank of inspector who is not involved in the investigation.

(b) Entry other than with consent

6.4 The officer in charge of the search shall first try to communicate with the occupier, or any other person entitled to grant access to the premises, explain the authority under which entry is sought and ask the occupier to allow entry, unless:

(i) the search premises are unoccupied;

(ii) the occupier and any other person entitled to grant access are absent;

(iii) there are reasonable grounds for believing that alerting the occupier or any other person entitled to grant access would frustrate the object of the search or endanger officers or other people.

6.5 Unless *sub-paragraph 6.4(iii)* applies, if the premises are occupied the officer, subject to *paragraph 2.9,* shall, before the search begins:

(i) identify him or herself, show their warrant card (if not in uniform) and state the purpose of, and grounds for, the search, and

(ii) identify and introduce any person accompanying the officer on the search (such persons should carry identification for production on request) and briefly describe that person's role in the process.

6.6 Reasonable and proportionate force may be used if necessary to enter premises if the officer in charge of the search is satisfied the premises are those specified in any warrant, or in exercise of the powers described in *paragraphs 4.1 to 4.3,* and if:

(i) the occupier or any other person entitled to grant access has refused entry;

(ii) it is impossible to communicate with the occupier or any other person entitled to grant access; or

(iii) any of the provisions of *paragraph 6.4* apply.

(c) Notice of Powers and Rights

6.7   If an officer conducts a search to which this Code applies the officer shall, unless it is impracticable to do so, provide the occupier with a copy of a Notice in a standard format:

(i)   specifying if the search is made under warrant, with consent, or in the exercise of the powers described in *paragraphs 4.1* to *4.3*. Note: the notice format shall provide for authority or consent to be indicated (see *paragraphs 4.3* and *5.1*);

(ii)   summarising the extent of the powers of search and seizure conferred by PACE and other relevant legislation as appropriate;

(iii) explaining the rights of the occupier and the owner of the property seized;

(iv)   explaining compensation may be payable in appropriate cases for damages caused entering and searching premises, and giving the address to send a compensation application (see *Note 6A*), and

(v)   stating this Code is available at any police station.

6.8   If the occupier is:

- present; copies of the Notice and warrant shall, if practicable, be given to them before the search begins, unless the officer in charge of the search reasonably believes this would frustrate the object of the search or endanger officers or other people;

- not present; copies of the Notice and warrant shall be left in a prominent place on the premises or appropriate part of the premises and endorsed, subject to *paragraph 2.9* with the name of the officer in charge of the search, the date and time of the search.

The warrant shall be endorsed to show this has been done.

(d) Conduct of searches

6.9   Premises may be searched only to the extent necessary to achieve the purpose of the search, having regard to the size and nature of whatever is sought.

6.9A   A search may not continue under:

- a warrant's authority once all the things specified in that warrant have been found;

- any other power once the object of that search has been achieved.

6.9B   No search may continue once the officer in charge of the search is satisfied whatever is being sought is not on the premises (see *Note 6B*). This does not prevent a further search of the same premises if additional grounds come to light supporting a further application for a search warrant or exercise or further exercise of another power. For example, when, as a result of new information, it is believed articles previously not found or additional articles are on the premises.

6.10   Searches must be conducted with due consideration for the property and privacy of the occupier and with no more disturbance than necessary. Reasonable force may be used only when necessary and proportionate because the co-operation of the occupier cannot be obtained or is insufficient for the purpose. (See *Note 6C*.)

6.11   A friend, neighbour or other person must be allowed to witness the search if the occupier wishes unless the officer in charge of the search has reasonable grounds for believing the presence of the person asked for would seriously hinder the investigation or endanger officers or other people. A search need not be unreasonably delayed for this purpose. A record of the action taken should be made on the premises search record including the grounds for refusing the occupier's request.

6.12   A person is not required to be cautioned prior to being asked questions that are solely necessary for the purpose of furthering the proper and effective conduct of a search, see Code C, *paragraph 10.1(c)*. For example, questions to discover the occupier of specified premises, to find a key to open a locked drawer or cupboard or to otherwise seek co-operation during the search or to determine if a particular item is liable to be seized.

6.12A   If questioning goes beyond what is necessary for the purpose of the exemption in Code C, the exchange is likely to constitute an interview as defined by Code C, *paragraph 11.1A* and would require the associated safeguards included in Code C, *section 10*.

(e) Leaving premises

6.13   If premises have been entered by force, before leaving the officer in charge of the search must make sure they are secure by:

- arranging for the occupier or their agent to be present;

- any other appropriate means.

(f) Searches under PACE Schedule 1 or the Terrorism Act 2000, Schedule 5

6.14   An officer shall be appointed as the officer in charge of the search (see *paragraph 2.10*), in respect of any search made under a warrant issued under PACE Act 1984, Schedule 1 or the Terrorism Act 2000, Schedule 5. They are responsible for making sure the search is conducted with discretion and in a manner that causes the least possible disruption to any business or other activities carried out on the premises.

6.15   Once the officer in charge of the search is satisfied material may not be taken from the premises without their knowledge, they shall ask for the documents or other records concerned. The officer in charge of the search may also ask to see the index to files held on the premises, and the officers conducting the search may inspect any files which, according to the index, appear to contain the material sought. A more extensive search of the premises may be made only if:

- the person responsible for them refuses to:
  - ~ produce the material sought, or
  - ~ allow access to the index.

- it appears the index is:
  - ~ inaccurate, or
  - ~ incomplete.

- for any other reason the officer in charge of the search has reasonable grounds for believing such a search is necessary in order to find the material sought.

Notes for guidance

6A   Whether compensation is appropriate depends on the circumstances in each case. Compensation for damage caused when effecting entry is unlikely to be appropriate if the search was lawful, and the force used can be shown to be reasonable, proportionate and necessary to effect entry. If the wrong premises are searched by mistake everything possible should be done at the earliest opportunity to allay any sense of grievance and there should normally be a strong presumption in favour of paying compensation.

6B   *It is important that, when possible, all those involved in a search are fully briefed about any powers to be exercised and the extent and limits within which it should be conducted.*

6C   *In all cases the number of officers and other persons involved in executing the warrant should be determined by what is reasonable and necessary according to the particular circumstances.*

7   Seizure and retention of property

(a) Seizure

7.1   Subject to *paragraph 7.2*, an officer who is searching any person or premises under any statutory power or with the consent of the occupier may seize anything:

(a) covered by a warrant;

(b) the officer has reasonable grounds for believing is evidence of an offence or has been obtained in consequence of the commission of an offence but only if seizure is necessary to prevent the items being concealed, lost, disposed of, altered, damaged, destroyed or tampered with;

(c) covered by the powers in the Criminal Justice and Police Act 2001, Part 2 allowing an officer to seize property from persons or premises and retain it for sifting or examination elsewhere.

See *Note 7B*

7.2   No item may be seized which an officer has reasonable grounds for believing to be subject to legal privilege, as defined in PACE, section 10, other than under the Criminal Justice and Police Act 2001, Part 2.

7.3   Officers must be aware of the provisions in the Criminal Justice and Police Act 2001, section 59, allowing for applications to a judicial authority for the return of property seized and the subsequent duty to secure in section 60. (See *paragraph 7.12(iii)*.)

7.4   An officer may decide it is not appropriate to seize property because of an explanation from the person holding it but may nevertheless have reasonable grounds for believing it was obtained in consequence of an offence by some person. In these circumstances, the officer should identify the property to the holder, inform the holder of their suspicions and explain the holder may be liable to civil or criminal proceedings if they dispose of, alter or destroy the property.

7.5   An officer may arrange to photograph, image or copy, any document or other article they have the power to seize in accordance with *paragraph 7.1*. This is subject to specific restrictions on the examination, imaging or copying of certain property seized under the Criminal Justice and Police Act 2001, Part 2. An officer must have regard to their statutory obligation to retain an original document or other article only when a photograph or copy is not sufficient.

7.6   If an officer considers information stored in any electronic form and accessible from the premises could be used in evidence, they may require the information to be produced in a form:

•   which can be taken away and in which it is visible and legible, or

•   from which it can readily be produced in a visible and legible form.

(b) Criminal Justice and Police Act 2001: Specific procedures for seize and sift powers

7.7　The Criminal Justice and Police Act 2001, Part 2 gives officers limited powers to seize property from premises or persons so they can sift or examine it elsewhere. Officers must be careful they only exercise these powers when it is essential and they do not remove any more material than necessary. The removal of large volumes of material, much of which may not ultimately be retainable, may have serious implications for the owners, particularly when they are involved in business or activities such as journalism or the provision of medical services. Officers must carefully consider if removing copies or images of relevant material or data would be a satisfactory alternative to removing originals. When originals are taken, officers must be prepared to facilitate the provision of copies or images for the owners when reasonably practicable. (See *Note 7C.*)

7.8　Property seized under the Criminal Justice and Police Act 2001, sections 50 or 51 must be kept securely and separately from any material seized under other powers. An examination under section 53 to determine which elements may be retained must be carried out at the earliest practicable time, having due regard to the desirability of allowing the person from whom the property was seized, or a person with an interest in the property, an opportunity of being present or represented at the examination.

7.8A　All reasonable steps should be taken to accommodate an interested person's request to be present, provided the request is reasonable and subject to the need to prevent harm to, interference with, or unreasonable delay to the investigatory process. If an examination proceeds in the absence of an interested person who asked to attend or their representative, the officer who exercised the relevant seizure power must give that person a written notice of why the examination was carried out in those circumstances. If it is necessary for security reasons or to maintain confidentiality officers may exclude interested persons from decryption or other processes which facilitate the examination but do not form part of it. (See *Note 7D.*)

7.9　It is the responsibility of the officer in charge of the investigation to make sure property is returned in accordance with sections 53 to 55. Material which there is no power to retain must be:

- separated from the rest of the seized property, and

- returned as soon as reasonably practicable after examination of all the seized property.

7.9A　Delay is only warranted if very clear and compelling reasons exist, for example:

- the unavailability of the person to whom the material is to be returned, or

- the need to agree a convenient time to return a large volume of material

7.9B　Legally privileged, excluded or special procedure material which cannot be retained must be returned:

- as soon as reasonably practicable, and

- without waiting for the whole examination.

7.9C　As set out in section 58, material must be returned to the person from whom it was seized, except when it is clear some other person has a better right to it. (See *Note 7E.*)

7.10   When an officer involved in the investigation has reasonable grounds to believe a person with a relevant interest in property seized under section 50 or 51 intends to make an application under section 59 for the return of any legally privileged, special procedure or excluded material, the officer in charge of the investigation should be informed as soon as practicable and the material seized should be kept secure in accordance with section 61. (See *Note 7C*.)

7.11   The officer in charge of the investigation is responsible for making sure property is properly secured. Securing involves making sure the property is not examined, copied, imaged or put to any other use except at the request, or with the consent, of the applicant or in accordance with the directions of the appropriate judicial authority. Any request, consent or directions must be recorded in writing and signed by both the initiator and the officer in charge of the investigation. (See *Notes 7F* and *7G*.)

7.12   When an officer exercises a power of seizure conferred by sections 50 or 51 they shall provide the occupier of the premises or the person from whom the property is being seized with a written notice:

(i)   specifying what has been seized under the powers conferred by that section;

(ii)   specifying the grounds for those powers;

(iii)   setting out the effect of sections 59 to 61 covering the grounds for a person with a relevant interest in seized property to apply to a judicial authority for its return and the duty of officers to secure property in certain circumstances when an application is made, and

(iv)   specifying the name and address of the person to whom:

- notice of an application to the appropriate judicial authority in respect of any of the seized property must be given;

- an application may be made to allow attendance at the initial examination of the property.

7.13   If the occupier is not present but there is someone in charge of the premises, the notice shall be given to them. If no suitable person is available, so the notice will easily be found it should either be:

- left in a prominent place on the premises, or

- attached to the exterior of the premises.

(c)   Retention

7.14   Subject to *paragraph 7.15*, anything seized in accordance with the above provisions may be retained only for as long as is necessary. It may be retained, among other purposes:

(i)   for use as evidence at a trial for an offence;

(ii)   to facilitate the use in any investigation or proceedings of anything to which it is inextricably linked (see *Note 7H*);

(iii)   for forensic examination or other investigation in connection with an offence;

(iv)   in order to establish its lawful owner when there are reasonable grounds for believing it has been stolen or obtained by the commission of an offence.

7.15   Property shall not be retained under *paragraph 7.14(i), (ii)* or *(iii)* if a copy or image would be sufficient.

(d) Rights of owners etc

7.16   If property is retained, the person who had custody or control of it immediately before seizure must, on request, be provided with a list or description of the property within a reasonable time.

7.17   That person or their representative must be allowed supervised access to the property to examine it or have it photographed or copied, or must be provided with a photograph or copy, in either case within a reasonable time of any request and at their own expense, unless the officer in charge of an investigation has reasonable grounds for believing this would:

(i)   prejudice the investigation of any offence or criminal proceedings; or

(ii)   lead to the commission of an offence by providing access to unlawful material such as pornography;

A record of the grounds shall be made when access is denied.

Notes for guidance

7A   *Any person claiming property seized by the police may apply to a magistrates' court under the Police (Property) Act 1897 for its possession and should, if appropriate, be advised of this procedure.*

7B   *The powers of seizure conferred by PACE, sections 18(2) and 19(3) extend to the seizure of the whole premises when it is physically possible to seize and retain the premises in their totality and practical considerations make seizure desirable. For example, police may remove premises such as tents, vehicles or caravans to a police station for the purpose of preserving evidence.*

7C   *Officers should consider reaching agreement with owners and/or other interested parties on the procedures for examining a specific set of property, rather than awaiting the judicial authority's determination. Agreement can sometimes give a quicker and more satisfactory route for all concerned and minimise costs and legal complexities.*

7D   *What constitutes a relevant interest in specific material may depend on the nature of that material and the circumstances in which it is seized. Anyone with a reasonable claim to ownership of the material and anyone entrusted with its safe keeping by the owner should be considered.*

7E   *Requirements to secure and return property apply equally to all copies, images or other material created because of seizure of the original property.*

7F   *The mechanics of securing property vary according to the circumstances; "bagging up", i.e. placing material in sealed bags or containers and strict subsequent control of access is the appropriate procedure in many cases.*

7G   *When material is seized under the powers of seizure conferred by PACE, the duty to retain it under the Code of Practice issued under the Criminal Procedure and Investigations Act 1996 is subject to the provisions on retention of seized material in PACE, section 22.*

7H   *Paragraph 7.14 (ii) applies if inextricably linked material is seized under the Criminal Justice and Police Act 2001, sections 50 or 51. Inextricably linked material is material it is not reasonably practicable to separate from other linked material without prejudicing the use of that other material in any investigation or proceedings. For example, it may not be possible to separate items of data held on computer disk without damaging their evidential integrity. Inextricably linked material must not be examined, imaged, copied or used for any purpose other than for proving the source and/or integrity of the linked material.*

8   **Action after searches**

8.1   If premises are searched in circumstances where this Code applies, unless the exceptions in *paragraph 2.3(a)* apply, on arrival at a police station the officer in charge of the search shall make or have made a record of the search, to include:

     (i)   the address of the searched premises;

     (ii)   the date, time and duration of the search;

     (iii)   the authority used for the search:

- if the search was made in exercise of a statutory power to search premises without warrant, the power which was used for the search:

- if the search was made under a warrant or with written consent;

     ~   a copy of the warrant and the written authority to apply for it, *see paragraph 3.4*; or

     ~   the written consent;

     shall be appended to the record or the record shall show the location of the copy warrant or consent;

     (iv)   subject to *paragraph 2.9*, the names of:

- the officer(s) in charge of the search;

- all other officers and authorised persons who conducted the search;

     (v)   the names of any people on the premises if they are known;

     (vi)   any grounds for refusing the occupier's request to have someone present during the search, see *paragraph 6.11;*

     (vii)   a list of any articles seized or the location of a list and, if not covered by a warrant, the grounds for their seizure;

     (viii)   whether force was used, and the reason;

     (ix)   details of any damage caused during the search, and the circumstances;

     (x)   if applicable, the reason it was not practicable;

        (a)   to give the occupier a copy of the Notice of Powers and Rights, see *paragraph 6.7*;

        (b)   before the search to give the occupier a copy of the Notice, see *paragraph 6.8;*

     (xi)   when the occupier was not present, the place where copies of the Notice of Powers and Rights and search warrant were left on the premises, see *paragraph 6.8.*

8.2   On each occasion when premises are searched under warrant, the warrant authorising the search on that occasion shall be endorsed to show:

(i)   if any articles specified in the warrant were found and the address where found;

(ii)   if any other articles were seized;

(iii)   the date and time it was executed and if present, the name of the occupier or if the occupier is not present the name of the person in charge of the premises;

(iv)   subject to *paragraph 2.9*, the names of the officers who executed it and any authorised persons who accompanied them, and

(v)   if a copy, together with a copy of the Notice of Powers and Rights was:

- handed to the occupier, or

- endorsed as required by *paragraph 6.8*; and left on the premises and where.

8.3   Any warrant shall be returned within three calendar months of its issue or sooner on completion of the search(es) authorised by that warrant, if it was issued by a:

- justice of the peace, to the designated officer for the local justice area in which the justice was acting when issuing the warrant; or

- judge, to the appropriate officer of the court concerned,

9   Search registers

9.1   A search register will be maintained at each sub-divisional or equivalent police station. All search records required under *paragraph 8.1* shall be made, copied, or referred to in the register. (See *Note 9A*.)

Note for guidance

9A   Paragraph 9.1 also applies to search records made by immigration officers. In these cases, a search register must also be maintained at an immigration office. (See also Note 2D.)

10   Searches under Schedule 5 to the Terrorism Prevention and Investigation Measures Act 2011.

10.1   This Code applies to the powers of constables under Schedule 5 to the Terrorism Prevention and Investigation Measures Act 2011 relating to TPIM notices to enter and search premises subject to the modifications in the following paragraphs.

10.2   In paragraph 2.3(d), the reference to the investigation into an alleged or suspected offence include the enforcement of terrorism prevention and investigation measures which may be imposed on an individual by a TPIM notice in accordance with the Terrorism Prevention and Investigation Measures Act 2011.

10.3   References to the purpose and object of the entry and search of premises, the nature of articles sought and what may be seized and retained include (as appropriate):

(a)   in relation to the power to search *without a search warrant* in *paragraph 5* (for purposes of serving TPIM notice), finding the individual on whom the notice is to be served.

(b)   in relation to the power to search *without a search warrant* in *paragraph 6* (at time of serving TPIM notice), ascertaining whether there is anything in the premises, that contravenes measures specified in the notice. (See *Note 10A*.)

(c)   in relation to the power to search *without a search warrant* under *paragraph 7* (suspected absconding), ascertaining whether a person has absconded or if there is anything on the premises which will assist in the pursuit or arrest of an individual in respect of whom a TPIM notice is force who is reasonably suspected of having absconded.

(d)   in relation to the power to search *under a search warrant* issued under *paragraph 8* (for compliance purposes), determining whether an individual in respect of whom a TPIM notice is in force is complying with measures specified in the notice. (See *Note 10A.)*

Note for guidance

10A   Searches of individuals under Schedule 5, paragraphs 6(2)(a) (at time of serving TPIM notice) and 8(2)(a) (for compliance purposes) must be conducted and recorded in accordance with Code A. See Code A paragraph 2.18A *for details.*